WORLDVIEW GUIDE

ADVENTURES *of* HUCKLEBERRY FINN

Douglas Wilson

canonpress
Moscow, Idaho

Published by Canon Press
P.O. Box 8729, Moscow, Idaho 83843
800.488.2034 | www.canonpress.com

Douglas Wilson, *Worldview Guide for Adventures of Huckleberry Finn,*
1st Ed. Revised.
Copyright ©2016 by Douglas Wilson.
Cited page numbers come from the Canon Classics edition of the novel (2016),
www.canonpress.com/books/canon-classics.

Cover design by James Engerbretson
Cover illustration by Forrest Dickison
Interior design by Valerie Anne Bost and James Engerbretson

Printed in the United States of America.

A free end-of-book test and answer key are available for download at
www.canonpress.com/ClassicsQuizzes

Library of Congress Cataloging-in-Publication Data
Wilson, Douglas, 1953- author.
Adventures of Huckleberry Finn / by Douglas Wilson.
Moscow, Idaho : Canon Press, 2016. | Series: Canon Classics
   Worldview Guide
LCCN 2016026824 | ISBN 9781944503413 (pbk. : alk. paper)
LCSH: Twain, Mark, 1835-1910. Adventures of Huckleberry
   Finn—Juvenile literature.
LCC PS1305 .W59 2016 | DDC 813/.4—dc23
LC record available at https://lccn.loc.gov/2016026824

16 17 18 19 20 21   9 8 7 6 5 4 3

CONTENTS

INTRODUCTION

Adventures of Huckleberry Finn is the best known book of Mark Twain, a preeminent American author. Fifty years after the publication of *Huck Finn*, the writer Earnest Hemingway declared that all distinctively American literature marks its descent from this story. It is the story of a boy named Huck escaping from "civilization" down the great Mississippi River with a runaway slave named Jim.

THE WORLD AROUND

Huckleberry Finn was published in the UK and Canada in 1884 (because of a publishing error, it came out in the U.S. the next year). What else was happening in the course of that year? A patent was given to John Kellogg for his new-fangled "flaked cereal." The cornerstone for the Statue of Liberty was laid. Grover Cleveland was elected president for his first term. The first World Series was played, in which the Mets lost to a team called Providence. Queen Victoria had been on the throne for almost forty years. The telephone had just recently been invented (in 1876). A few years later, in 1900, when Winston Churchill was only 26 and beginning a lecture tour in America, he was introduced by none other than Mark Twain.

ABOUT THE AUTHOR

Samuel Langhorne Clemens was born in Missouri in 1835. His pen name was Mark Twain, and was taken from his brief stint as a riverboat pilot as a young man. On the riverboats, *mark twain* (meaning "mark #2") indicated they had sounded a depth of twelve feet, or two fathoms. This was deep enough for a steamboat—an important piece of information for those on steamboats.

Twain lived from 1835 to 1910. Both the year of his birth and the year of his death were marked by an appearance of Halley's Comet, which moves in a seventy-five or seventy-six year orbit. Twain was born shortly after the comet appeared, and he predicted he "would go out with it" too. When the comet appeared again, Twain died the next day. A humorist has to understand the importance of timing.

Although he was known as a quintessential American humorist, he was also a deeply cynical man, and not least about himself. He would refer to the "damned human race," but he was not criticizing from outside. He included himself fully as part of the problem. He was an unbeliever, and wrote about that unbelief in detail—but stipulated that it not be published until well after his death.

At the same time, he displayed remarkable honesty of character in some instances. He once went bankrupt as a result of some bad investments, and after he recovered his footing, he paid off all his creditors—even though he had no legal obligation to do so.

WHAT OTHER
NOTABLES SAID

H.L. Mencken had this to say about how American the book is: "But in *Huckleberry Finn*, in *A Connecticut Yankee* and in most of the short sketches there is a quality that is unmistakably and overwhelmingly national. They belong to our country and our time quite as obviously as the skyscraper or the quick lunch counter. They are as magnificently American as the Brooklyn Bridge or Tammany Hall."[1]

T.S. Eliot wrote an introduction to the work in which he described it as a work of genius—and Eliot ought to know. "*The Adventures of Huckleberry Finn* is the only one of Mark Twain's various books which can be called a masterpiece. I do not suggest that it is his only book of

---

1.   H.L. Mencken, "Mark Twain's Americanism," in Harold Bloom, ed., *Bloom's Classic Critical Views: Mark Twain* (New York: Infobase, 2009).

permanent interest; but it is the only one in which his genius is completely realized, and the only one which creates its own category."[2]

And, as mentioned in the introduction, Ernest Hemingway was enthusiastic about the book. Here is the precise quote. "All modern American literature comes from one book by Mark Twain called *Huckleberry Finn*. American writing comes from that. There was nothing before. There has been nothing as good since."[3]

---

2. T.S. Eliot, "Introduction to Huckleberry Finn," in *Adventures of Huckleberry Finn* (London: Cresset, 1950), vii–xvi.

3. Ernest Hemingway, *Green Hills of Africa*, (New York: Scribner, 1935), 22.

PLOT SUMMARY, SETTING, AND CHARACTERS

- *Setting: the Mississippi River in the 1830s*
- *Huckleberry Finn:* a boy running from his dad
- *Jim:* a man running from slavery
- *Tom Sawyer:* Huck's clever best friend
- *Aunt Polly and Aunt Sally:* Tom's aunts
- *The Duke and the King:* two con men who use Huck and Jim
- *Widow Douglas and Miss Watson:* Jim's owner and her sister who want to civilize Huck
- *Pap Finn:* Huck's hard-drinking father
- *Grangerfords and Shepherdsons:* two feuding families of the Old South
- *the Wilks girls:* heiresses of a large fortune

The story begins in St. Petersburg, Missouri. At the end of Tom Sawyer, Tom and Huck Finn had come into a goodly amount of money, having discovered a robber's stash. As a result, the bank was holding Huck's money for him in trust, and he was adopted by the Widow Douglas, a situation which, despite the widow's kindness, he found to be stifling. Widow Douglas lived with her sister, Miss Watson.

Huck is dealing with it until his father, Pap Finn, a brutish drunk, appears and demands the money. Pap eventually kidnaps Huck, and holds him across the river from St. Petersburg. Huck escapes by faking his own death, and spends a few days on an island in the middle of the river. There he runs into the other main character of the novel, a runaway slave named Jim. He belonged to Miss Watson, and had heard that he was going to be sold down the river, and separated from his wife and children. Huck and Jim decide to team up.

As a result of a great storm, the river floods and Huck and Jim see a raft and a house floating by. They commandeer the raft, and loot the house. In that house they find a dead body of a man who had been shot. Jim won't let Huck see the man's face. Afraid that their hiding place on the island has been figured out, they decide to head downriver. The plan is to float to the confluence of the Mississippi and the Ohio, and then to head upstream on the Ohio by steamboat to the free states.

After various adventures, they float past the Ohio accidentally. After a steamboat rams their raft, Jim and Huck are separated. Huck spends a short time in the middle of a feud between the Grangerfords and Shepherdsons, and when Jim shows up with the repaired raft, they make their escape again. They then happen to rescue a couple of con artists (calling themselves the duke and the king), and have various adventures as a result of attempted scams perpetrated by these homeless aristocrats. The two scoundrels crown their misbehavior by selling Jim to a farmer, telling him that Jim is a runaway, for whom a significant reward was offered.

Things pick up. Huck resolves to rescue Jim. The family holding Jim were Tom Sawyer's uncle and aunt. They mistake Huck for Tom because Tom was due to visit. Huck plays along with the mistake, and catches Tom before he gets there to fill him in. Tom identifies himself as his own younger brother going by the name of Sid. Tom concocts a major adventure out of the relatively easy task of freeing Jim. As a result, Tom is shot in the leg and they are all taken into custody.

Tom then reveals that the whole thing was unnecessary because Miss Watson had died a few months before, and there was a provision in her will freeing Jim. Tom's Aunt Polly arrives and reveals that Tom and Sid are actually Huck and Tom. Huck is afraid his father will show up and ruin everything, and so Jim reveals to him that the dead man in the floating house had been Huck's father. Aunt Sally offers to adopt Huck, but he decides that he would rather head out West.

WORLDVIEW ANALYSIS

You probably saw the "Notice" Mark Twain put at the start of his book: "Persons attempting to find a motive in this narrative will be prosecuted; persons attempting to find a moral in it will be banished; persons attempting to find a plot in it will be shot" (p. iv). If by this warning Twain meant that you should refrain from the allegory of woodenly turning Huck into "all humans" and the River into the River of Life or "God" (as some have done), then we can agree with him: don't do that. But if Twain was hinting that *Huck Finn* had no worldview or deeper meaning in it whatsoever, then he was trying to pull the wool over your eyes—because no great stories are shallow.

The great central climax of *Huck Finn* occurs after the duke and king double-cross Jim by selling him to the Phelpses for $40 (which would be somewhere around $1,160 today). Huck is trying to figure out what to do, and he begins to reflect on the lessons he had been taught on helping runaway slaves. A person who behaved the way he had been behaving "goes to everlasting fire."

And so as a consequence Huck has a moral crisis, and he decides to write to Miss Watson, Jim's original owner, to tell her where Jim is to be found. Once he made this decision, this is how it all played out.

> I felt good and all washed clean of sin for the first time I had ever felt so in my life, and I knowed I could pray now. But I didn't do it straight off, but laid the paper down and set there thinking—thinking how good it was all this happened so, and how near I come to being lost and going to hell. And went on thinking. And got to thinking over our trip down the river; and I see Jim before me, all the time; in the day, and in the night-time, sometimes moonlight, sometimes storms, and we a floating along, talking, and singing, and laughing. But somehow I couldn't seem to strike no places to harden me against him, but only the other kind. I'd see him standing my watch on top of his'n, stead of calling me, so I could go on sleeping; and see him how glad he was when I come back out of the fog; and when I come to him agin in the swamp, up there where the feud was; and such-like times; and would always call me honey, and pet me, and do everything he could think of for me, and how good he always was; and at last I struck the time I saved him by telling the men we had smallpox aboard, and he was so grateful, and said I was the best friend old Jim ever had in the world, and the *only* one he's got now; and then I happened to look around, and see that paper. (Ch. XXXI, p. 232–3)

This is the moment of truth in the novel, and Huck's destiny rides on it.

> It was a close place. I took it up, and held it in my hand. I was a trembling, because I'd got to decide, forever, betwixt two things, and I knowed it. I studied a minute, sort of holding my breath, and then says to myself: 'All right, then, I'll *go* to hell'—and tore it up. (Ch. XXXI, p. 233)

Rather than do the wrong thing and go to Heaven, Huck decides in effect to do the right thing and go to Hell: "It was awful thoughts, and awful words, but they was said. And I let them stay said; and never thought no more about reforming."

Now we should not be too hard on Huck for several reasons. The first is that he is just a poorly taught boy and did not know what he was doing. The second reason is that he is a fictional poorly taught boy, and that means that if we have to find fault, it should be with Mark Twain, who *did* know what he was doing.

Notice how Twain sets Huck (and us) up. Huck enters into a state of moral cleansing and he knows that he "could pray now." He was "washed clean of sin for the first time." The cost of admission into this blessed state was simply that of becoming treacherous, betraying a poor runaway slave. Huck had to become a terrible human being—that is all a holy God required of him.

So Huck turns his back on this option, eventually getting to the point where he would think "no more about reforming." No more paths of righteousness for him—he was going to be *wicked*.

Now obviously, Twain is not trying to make us think that there really is a God, and that this God actually rewards cruel slave masters who ply the lash to their victims, and that He punishes small boys who try to help such slaves get away. He is trying to show us a young boy caught up in a sinful system, which he nevertheless *believes* to be righteous, but which he still revolts against on a deeper instinctive level.

This point, so far as it goes, is genuinely powerful, and Twain could have made it more powerful still. But as it stands, Twain just plays a cheap trick on the reader. If Huck had come to the realization that "there *has* to be a deeper right than the 'right' I have been taught," and he had then determined to follow that true right whatever the cost, then we could have a genuinely moving scene—instead of what we actually have, which is an atheistic card trick.

In Twain's literary assumption here, there is no *functional* God. (I am leaving out of the discussion whether or not Twain was a true *bona fide* atheist. He is frequently touted by atheists as being one of them, but it might not be quite that simple. There are places where he seemed to leave room for the existence of a God, or even the possibility of an afterlife.) But in the dilemma he creates for Huck in this scene, he is operating on the basis of a functional unbelief. God, if He exists, does not appear to be relevant to this situation.

So all we have is the false system of morality that Huck was taught, and when we walk away from that, if we have no alternative, nothing waits ahead of us but . . . the abyss.

What do I mean? It means that, in Twain's world, the slave master's crime is not in how he treats his slaves, but rather in the fact that he appeals to a non-existent God to justify it. And even there we are talking about an error in fact, which is not the same thing as a sin or a crime.

If there is a Heaven and Hell such as Huck imagines, then we have a perverse cosmos indeed. Compassionate boys go to Hell and cruel and vindictive slave masters go to Heaven. But according to Twain, there is no such system of perverse justice in the afterlife because we have no positive ground for believing in an afterlife at all.

So where is Huck choosing to go then? He is choosing to go into an absurd nothingness, just like everyone else. In other words, the whole human race—Jim, Huck, Becky Thatcher, Pap Finn, Tom Sawyer, Miss Watson, the whole lot—are all in the same absurd position.

If there is such a thing as true justice, then what is it? *And how can we know?* If there is no such thing as justice, then there is nothing wrong with Huck running off with Jim. But neither is there anything wrong with the duke and king selling Jim for $40.

If justice exists, then everyone has a duty to find out what it is in order to pursue it. If it does not exist, then it doesn't much matter what direction we go—everything is simply aimless anyway.

Mark Twain is caught in the grip of a true dilemma, one which all unbelievers face, and for which there is no effective answer. You cannot use standards of righteousness derived from Christianity in order to discredit Christianity *in toto*, because what you have done is discredit that standard of judgment you have been using. You not only kill the victim Christianity, but you also destroy the weapon with which you killed it.

You took a sword from Christianity in order to slay the false religion of Christianity. But when you have slain it, you discover that the sword you used has itself dissolved into a vapor and can't kill anything.

Turning Jim in is either right or wrong. If it is right, then Huck should do it. If it is wrong, then he shouldn't do it. But in order to make such weighty decisions, we need much more than a young boy's instinctive feeling that he ought to obey his innate "conscience" while defiantly disobeying his trained conscience. Because for Huck, all the *ought* fell on the side of his trained conscience and the motive force for his innate conscience didn't seem to him like conscience at all. He simply felt that he did not want to betray Jim because of how Jim had been so kind to him. When Huck stayed with Jim as he did, he was not doing so out of any sense of duty at all. All the duty was pressing him in the other direction.

But what "goes away" now that we have abandoned obedience to duty? Obedience to duty, incidentally, includes figuring out whatever false obligations I may have taken on myself and rejecting them. But if I simply decide that I don't *feel* like fulfilling a false obligation and therefore walk away from *all* obligations (because I have now opted for Hell), I will discover soon enough that my only standard is one that I share with Miss Watson ... and with Pap Finn. "What do I *feel* like doing?"

Some people feel like owning slaves. Others feel like running away from their masters. Some people want to help them run away. Others want to teach Sunday School lessons that instruct young people on how bad it would be to help a slave run away. One of the fundamental realities of true moral thinking has to be the realization that the standard, the law, the code, of righteousness not only has to be outside of us, but it also must be *outside of the world.*

If morality is contained within this world that means that we can get at it. We can tinker with it, adjust it, or make it more to our liking. True morality is outside the created order, and this means that we can only do one of two things with it. We can conform to it, or we can rebel against it. If we rebel against it, we may pretend that we are conforming to it (by, say, mistreating a slave while praising the name of Jesus), but this is simply a higher form of rebellion.

Mark Twain *knows* that hypocrisy is wrong, which is why he is so merciless in his treatment of it. But if hypocrisy is wrong, it is failing against a higher standard. It is failing to conform to the standard that is outside the world. But why would a man reject the God of Heaven (He who is outside the world) because of the behavior of hypocrites who are also rejecting that very same God?

There are different ways of putting this, and they are all very important. If there is a hypocrite between you and God, then you are too far away from God. If there is a hypocrite between you and God, then why are you letting a hypocrite be closer to God than you are? Hypocrisy is counterfeit righteousness. The real thing is in Heaven. If a man hates hypocrisy, then he should love Jesus—who also hated hypocrisy.

If a man counterfeited gold coins, then it would be folly for someone else to throw away all his genuine gold coins because of the mere existence of the counterfeits. The existence of so many false Christians, for someone who is thinking carefully, should make one desperately want to be a true Christian. The reason for this should be obvious. If there are two sides, with God on one side and the hypocrites on the other, what sense does it make for me to go join the hypocrites because I hate hypocrisy so much? But to say that because a hypocrite is far away from God, and then to use that as an argument for staying far away from God yourself, is to fall into a bitter and very lonely trap. It is one that Mark Twain did in fact fall into.

There are many admirable things about Twain. He was a gifted writer. He was genuinely funny, a true humorist. He perfected the quintessential and very laconic American humor of the frontier. He created memorable characters. He was a memorable character. But when all is said and done, it has to be admitted that Mark Twain did not know God . . . and it showed.

QUOTABLES

1. "Persons attempting to find a motive in this narrative will be prosecuted; persons attempting to find a moral in it will be banished; persons attempting to find a plot in it will be shot."

    ~ Mark Twain, Notice (p. IV)

2. "After supper she got out her book and learned me about Moses and the Bulrushers, and I was in a sweat to find out all about him; but by and by she let it out that Moses had been dead a considerable long time; so then I didn't care no more about him, because I don't take no stock in dead people."

    ~ Huck, Chapter I (p. 2)

3. "It was a close place. I took it up [the note betraying Jim], and held it in my hand. I was a trembling, because I'd got to decide, forever, betwixt two things, and I knowed it. I studied a minute, sort of holding my breath, and then says to myself: 'All right, then, I'll *go* to

hell'—and tore it up. It was awful thoughts, and awful words, but they was said. And I let them stay said; and never thought no more about reforming."

~ Huck, Chapter XXXI (p. 233)

4. Well, it made me sick to see it [the King and the Duke being tarred and feathered]; and I was sorry for them poor pitiful rascals, it seemed like I couldn't ever feel any hardness against them any more in the world. It was a dreadful thing to see. Human beings *can* be awful cruel to one another."

~ Huck, Chapter XXXIII (p. 251–2)

5. "If I had a yaller dog that didn't know no more than a person's conscience does I would pison him."

~ Huck, Chapter XXXIII (p. 252)

6. "But I reckon I got to light out for the Territory ahead of the rest, because Aunt Sally she's going to adopt me and sivilize me, and I can't stand it. I been there before. THE END. YOURS TRULY, HUCK FINN."

~ Chapter XLIII (p. 318)

21 SIGNIFICANT
QUESTIONS AND ANSWERS

1. What are we to make of Twain's assertion in his introductory "Notice" that the novel had no deeper meaning?[4]

> We may take it seriously if we read him as meaning that the story is not a detailed allegory, where the Mississippi represents the river of life, and so on. But we can't take it seriously at all if he is claiming that there is no worldview carried by this book, or embodied by it. Well-told stories about human life always have a deeper meaning because human life has a deeper meaning. It is not possible to tell a good story that is shallow.

---

4. Remember, the five elements of a story are Setting, Characters, Plot, Conflict, and Themes (depending on whom you ask). Understanding each element is a key to appreciating the novel as a whole.

2. What are the basic differences between Tom Sawyer
    and Huck Finn as characters?

    > Tom is an adventurous boy who will eventually be
    > civilized, and Huck is a calmer soul who will not be.

3. Are there any consistent Christians in the novel?

    > The Widow Douglas. Maybe. Everyone else is
    > caught up in wild hypocrisy.

4. What does Twain think of slavery?

    > He hates it. The entire book is a dedicated effort to
    > undermine it.

5. Is Twain to be dismissed as a racist because the word
    "nigger" is used throughout the book?

    > Not at all. The students need to be brought to
    > understand that words often change their conno-
    > tations, sometimes dramatically, over the course of
    > years. Learning this is part of what it means to be
    > educated.

6. At the same time, now that the connotations of the
    word are much more offensive than they were when
    the book was published, what should we do about it?
    Should we use the word casually in our discussion of
    this book, for example?

When a word is deeply offensive to a large group of people, Christians should never use that word lightly. It is easy for us to say today that the word was in common use in polite society back then, and we can point out it did not have the same malicious connotations that it would have today in the mouth of a white person. This is partially true, but one of the reasons why the word was acceptable in white circles back then is that nobody cared about whether it was acceptable in black circles. In class discussions, be careful to speak charitably—whether you use a circumlocution like the "n-word" or not.

7.   What is the pivotal moment in the book?

The pivotal moment comes when Huck overcomes his conscience, and decides not to betray Jim. He decides to go to Hell rather than do the wrong thing by Jim.

8.   What is wrong with Huck's reasoning in this?

We should try to answer the question without picking on Huck. After all, he is just a boy in a bad jam, and he is also fictional. That said, it would be appropriate to answer what Twain is doing here. He sets up a "situation ethics" kind of bind for Huck, in which he sins deeply if he turns Jim in, and in which he believes himself to be sinning if he doesn't turn him in. He is bound by a false conscience, and decides to do the right thing even though it will send him to Hell.

9. What is wrong with what Twain is doing here?

> He is not setting the choice before us honestly. He
> is having Huck say, *"If turning Jim in is wrong, I
> don't want to be right."* That is fine as far as it goes,
> but it really doesn't go very far. All sorts of unan-
> swered questions are begging to be answered, and
> Twain simply skims over them all. He has Huck
> do something that every reader would sympathize
> with, but leaves him with absolutely no basis for
> doing the right thing the next time.

10. How is that?

> Huck chooses to go to Hell rather than do wrong.
> This means that he has accepted the view that a
> moral tyrant has complete control of who goes
> to Hell. If the answer comes back that Huck was
> simply choosing to go to the Hell he had been
> falsely taught about by the hypocritical Christians
> all around him, this still won't do. Their teaching
> was false either because there is no God, no Hell,
> etc. or their teaching was false because there is a
> Hell that is righteously governed. Twain did not
> believe in a God who governed the universe justly.
> That explains why he does not steer the reader into
> an understanding that should have understood that
> his refusal to betray Jim was not wrong at all. But
> if there is no God, no final right and wrong, what
> would have been wrong with Huck—if he had felt
> like it—turning Jim in? What was wrong with Pap
> treating Huck the way he did?

11. The book has been banned off and on since its first
    publication. Why?

> Initially, it was because the language throughout
> the book was vulgar and low, and the book was also
> pretty violent. The vulgarity that was objected to did
> include an objection to the word "nigger," but not
> because it was insulting to black Americans. The
> concern was more that it was insulting to the refined
> sensibilities of the readers. Objections over the possi-
> ble insult that it offered to the black community did
> not begin until much later—until the 1950s. But that
> concern has grown steadily up to the present.

12. Should *Adventures of Huckleberry Finn* be banned or
    boycotted?

> From the beginning, this book has been opposed
> by some group or another. In the early years some
> wanted to ban it because of the use of slang. As
> mentioned, in recent times, some of the efforts
> were because of the racial issues (and free use of
> the word "nigger"). Today Christians could object
> to it on theological grounds, because Twain sets up
> a false dilemma for Huck (discussed above). But
> Christians shouldn't ever support book bans like
> that. Rather, we should read such books and learn
> how to answer them.

13. What do Huck and Jim have in common?

> They both occupy the lower rungs of the society
> they live in. Jim is a black slave and Huck is "poor

white trash." They are both consistently at the mercy of others, with the threat of losing their freedom. The story is told from the vantage point of a vulnerable boy, which enables him (and the reader) to empathize with the vulnerability of the slave. They are both in the same boat, or to say it with greater precision, they were both on the same raft.

14. What else?

They are both runaways. Huck is running away from his abusive father. Jim is running away from slavery, and the parallel means that we are being guided into thinking that the system of slavery (and the country that perpetuated it) were also an "abusive father." In the analogy, the United States was Pap Finn.

15. How does Mark Twain use dialect in this story?

Reading something in dialect means that you face all the same challenges that dialect can present when you encounter it in real life—you feel like you got a taste of the "real" wherever it is you are, but you also have trouble understanding what is going on. In *Huck Finn*, the dialectic tends to reveal class structures more than regional accents. Huck and Jim both display a very rough and uneducated way of speaking as compared to someone like Tom. That communicates something about where the speakers are eventually going to wind up in society.

You also might have noticed that this book's
title is *Adventures of Huckleberry Finn,* as opposed
to the more proper first book, *The Adventures of
Tom Sawyer.* This is of course because *Adventures of
Huckleberry Finn* is told in Huck's voice, and Huck
doesn't care about definite articles.

16. What does the river symbolize?

It is complicated (symbolism doesn't reduce to
simple, one-to-one correlations as allegory does),
but the river is all about the promise of freedom.
And initially, it seems to fulfill that promise—they
can just float and smoke. But as the novel pro-
gresses, all sorts of threats to their freedom arise.
Life on the banks of the river starts to crowd in on
them. And on top of that, rivers eventually arrive
somewhere, and then you have to do something
particular. The novel ends with Huck deciding
to go "out West," which shimmers with the same
kind of elusive promise.

17. What is incomplete about Huck's decision to avoid
Heaven because that was where Miss Watson was going?
Given the kind of thing that made her happy, he "couldn't
see no advantage in going where she was going."

He doesn't apply the same consideration to those
he believes to be going to Hell. For example, he
wanted to stay away from Pap Finn in this life—he
ran away from him, after all—so why wouldn't he

want to stay away from him in the next? Is Heaven
the only place with poor company?

18. What is the overall tone of the book?

The novel should be considered satiric. In satire, wit
and barbed humor are used to expose and deflate
moral stupidity, vice, and hypocritical folly. Once an
effective satirist has had his way with a target, it is
very difficult to look at it the same way ever again.

19. What changes in the representation of Jim over the
course of this book?

When we first get to know him, he is represented
as superstitious and ignorant. This may be because
Twain is showing him to us through Huck's eyes—
with Huck sharing the stereotypical thinking of the
time. At the same time, Twain makes it clear that
Huck is also superstitious and ignorant. Later in the
novel, Jim shows great nobility in his behavior—after Tom is shot, for example.

20. Later in the book, what turns out to be ironic about the
flight of both Jim and Huck?

They were both fleeing from an imaginary threat.
Huck was fleeing from his father, who turned out
to be the dead man in the floating house, and Jim
was fleeing from Miss Watson, who had also died
and had set him free in her will.

21. What is the point of a grounded riverboat named
    Walter Scott?

> This also is part of Twain's satiric edge. He believed
> that the romanticism that was pervasive in the
> South (due in part to Sir Walter Scott's fiction) was
> one of the things that had crippled that culture.
> Twain actually believed that Scott's fiction was one
> of the causes of the Civil War. In this book he sim-
> ply places that approach to the world "on the rocks."

FURTHER DISCUSSION
AND REVIEW

Master what you have read by reviewing and integrating the five elements of this classic.

SETTING AND CHARACTERS
Be able to compare and contrast the personalities (including strengths, weaknesses, and mannerisms) of each character. How does the setting affect the characters?

PLOT
Be able to describe the beginning, middle, and end of the book along with specific details that move the plot forward and make it compelling. This includes the success or downfall (or both) of each character.

CONFLICT
Go through the character list and describe the tension between any and all main characters. Then, think about

whether any characters have internal conflict (in their own minds). Is there any overt conflict (fighting), or conflict with impersonal forces?

THEMES

Be able to describe what this classic is telling us about the world. Is the message true? What truth can we take from the plot, characters, conflict, and themes (even if the author didn't believe that truth)? Do any objects take on added meaning because of repetition or their place in the story (i.e., do any objects become symbols)? Be able to explain the following themes (or any others you've noticed) in this classic:

- slavery and freedom
- Romanticism and nobility
- hypocrisy
- moral stupidity and vice
- conscience and law
- disguise and counterfeit
- God and Heaven and Hell
- satire and humor
- civilization
- the Mississippi River

A NOTE FROM THE PUBLISHER:
TAKING THE CLASSICS QUIZ

Once you have finished the worldview guide, you can prepare for the end-of-book test. Each test will consist of a short-answer section on the book itself and the author, a short-answer section on plot and the narrative, and a long-answer essay section on worldview, conflict, and themes.

Each quiz, along with other helps, can be downloaded for free at www.canonpress.com/ClassicsQuizzes. If you have any questions about the quiz or its answers or the Worldview Guides in general, you can contact Canon Press at service@canonpress.com or 208.892.8074.

ABOUT THE AUTHOR

Douglas Wilson has been a pastor of Christ Church in Moscow, Idaho for forty years. He has started both a K-12 Christian school and an accredited Christian college, and has written more than fifty books. He and his wife Nancy have three children, all of whom have written books of their own, and he is the grandfather to a bunch of grandchildren.